DR. Ruch
Do Not
Remoue

D1541899

# FRANK LLOYD WRIGHT'S GUGGENHEIM MUSEUM

FRANK LLOYD WRIGHT'S GUGGENHEIM MUSEUM

# An Architectural Appreciation

edited by STEPHEN ROBERT FRANKEL

# FOREWORD

The influence of Frank Lloyd Wright (1867–1959) has been felt by architects worldwide ever since his work was published and exhibited in Germany in 1910. Speaking in 1946, Mies van der Rohe proclaimed, "Here finally was a master-builder drawing upon the veritable fountainhead of architecture. . . . Here, again, at last, genuine organic architecture flowered." Wright was praised by other modern architects throughout his career, and has found many fans among new generations. As Philip Johnson once said, "He is the type of genius that comes only once every three or four hundred years." This book presents quotes from architects and architecture historians about the Guggenheim Museum, perhaps the crowning achievement of Wright's life, together with photographs that convey some of these ideas.

—S.R.F.

The Guggenheim Museum represents the manifestation of the search for an expression of liberty, an architectural ideal, where the lyric and poetic transcend space and form. **Its unmistakably original silhouette, in the context of Manhattan, was a challenge to the architecture of its time**, and it remains today absolute and transcendental.

—Santiago Calatrava Valls, architect, Paris

The Guggenheim is a masterpiece of spatial flourish that confirms Frank Lloyd Wright's position as America's greatest architect. Didn't he say he was? And he was right. He is the greatest of all time but not of our time; within the context of now we can't but define his museum as architecture that subsumes the art in it—the Emersonian individuality of which dominates its occupants to make them ironic conformists, and the organic unity of which provides harmony via a **motival consistency that is as dominating and pretty as that harmony characteristic of Rococo architecture**.

—Robert Venturi, architect, Philadelphia

A grand gesture by a great master, who cocked a snoot at New York, its architects, and the Guggenheim art. Standing against the geometry of the private city around it, the building claims a place in the public realm and makes common cause with the park. **Its "bad fit" with New York is good—so long as it's the only one.** Inside, the central space makes the ceremony of enjoying the art as important as the art.

—Denise Scott Brown, architect, Philadelphia

I remember arriving in 1966 in New York as a student formed by the architecture of Europe. I discovered the skyscrapers, Central Park, and the Guggenheim Museum as three perfect elements responding to one another. With the **floating, expanding spiral, this eruption of a conic form within the quadrangular American city**, Frank Lloyd Wright introduces the architecture for the end of the century, offering New York its most efficient monument. He, who did not like the city, invents at the end of his life a modern interpretation of the relationship between exceptional buildings and the urban fabric.

—Christian de Portzamparc, architect, Paris

What the Guggenheim does is what all public buildings are supposed to do: distinguish itself from the fabric that they are in. . . . The churches, the public libraries, the museums, the monuments all stand out against the background. And **Wright understood that a great museum had to stand out from its environment, had to challenge the idea of the vertical surface—challenge the relationship to the park, to the corner, all of these things**. He produced a masterful work that challenged how we look at architecture, how we look at the museum, challenged curators to install things in different ways, provoked so many issues. And that's what architecture does in the end, and Wright understood this—it doesn't solve problems, it provokes new problems. . . . and that's what the greatness of architecture is, and that's what the greatness of this museum is.

—Peter Eisenman, architect, New York City

The Guggenheim Museum stands in inside-out upside-down geometric opposition to the gridded, boxed, stepped-back architecture of Manhattan. Yet Frank Lloyd Wright's defiant spatial creation differs from the defiant statement of other architects. **One senses, in the inner shape, the soul of a Zen Master who asks a final question in a coil of light and space**... in teleological suspension.

—Stephen Holl, architect, New York City

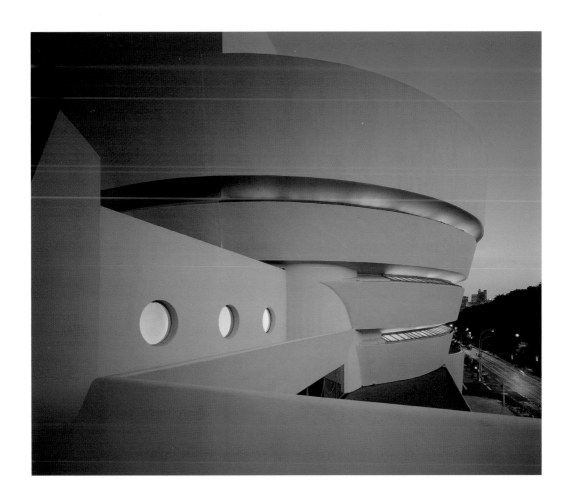

The Guggenheim Museum is twice removed from its gridlocked site on upper Fifth Avenue: once as a critique, and again as an alternative space. It operates in the spatio-temporal realm where utopia has always existed—"nowhere unless everywhere," as Wright liked to say—the realm of the imaginary and the fantastic. . . . For better or for worse—and Wright himself . . . would sense the problematic nature of the case— the Guggenheim Museum was never designed to have more than an abstract relationship with the city block on which it sits. The utopian program and its formal exegesis precluded all extrinsic concerns. The imaginary site at the beginning of the process subsumed the real one in the end.

Organic architecture was still the only true modern architecture for Wright by the last decade of his life . . . *Organic* refers to the relationships of parts to wholes, connoting integral and intrinsic qualities. . . . *Romance* stands for the creative force expressed by the inspired individual and the embodiment of poetry in form. *Tradition* does not require imitation of precedent, but a sense of belonging, as a robin belongs to a genus of birds. *Ornament* is the making of poetry, an emotional expression that is integrated into architecture and reveals and enhances the structure of building. *Spirit* is the essential life force within an object, not the imposition of a divine presence on high. . . . And *space* is the "continual becoming: invisible fountain from which all rhythms flow to which they must pass. Beyond time or infinity. The new reality which organic architecture serves to employ in building. The breath of a work of art."

—Anthony Alofsin, architecture historian

There is nothing in this building that is not inextricably connected. . . . every detail, no matter how insignificant, is an integral part in making up the whole building.

—Richard Meier, architect, New York City

The dominant, the unforgettable feature [of the Museum] is the circular central court of the larger tower surrounded by its six stories of spiraling ramps: "a light-flooded cathedral with a roadway to heaven winding round its walls."

John Coolidge, *Patrons and Architects*

Certain geometric forms have come to symbolize for us and potently to suggest certain human ideas, moods, and sentiments—as for instance: the circle, infinity; the triangle, structural unity; the spire, aspiration; the spiral, organic progress; the square, integrity.

—Frank Lloyd Wright, 1912

The Guggenheim is not merely a dazzling structure thrown over a flat floor plane; nor a sculptural fantasy for special effect. . . . [I]t posits **a curved space making itself into a building out of its climb and curvature, with floors, wall, and roof all integrally of the process**. It creates a kind of architectural experience for which scant precedent exists, and none in any such monumental statement. In these respects, no building of the mid-twentieth century more bravely challenges the future.

—William H. Jordy, architecture historian

Sometime between the early and middle decades of the twentieth century, the concept of the "museum of modern art" as just a plain white cube came into being, with just a simple floor to put the three-dimensional object and simple white walls to hang the two-dimensional art. If a gallery satisfies these two conditions, then people think this is the best gallery for modern art. And, in effect, it is just a very simple kind of loft, which is a bourgeois living room. A cold, plain, simple space. Frank Lloyd Wright had a completely different idea. He created extraordinary spaces.

Wright's spiral was: a contour traced in a dream, brought back intact from his own geography. What else but a building brought back from a dream would be windowless, have walls and floors and tilt and twist, begin on the top floor, spiral in toward the center like an enigma? . . . If in architecture the American scale of space had been successfully captured only by the skyscraper and the highway, the Guggenheim's interior held its own with both by turning the scale upside down and inward. The defensively introspective impulse that in [Wright's] Los Angeles houses had produced fortresses of gloom here was transfigured as it broke through recklessly into the Guggenheim's sun-splashed rotunda: cascading light, a wishing-well fountain, the pleasure garden of a mind liberated at last from the compulsion to make Organic Architecture intelligible in any language save its own sensuous form.

Wright was the heir, in architecture—and regarded himself as being so—of a tradition, in part Jeffersonian, which had previously found its best expression in the works of Melville, Whitman, and Mark Twain. As they, in their writing, had celebrated at once the flux and flow which characterize modern times and the compulsion toward unity which is the democratic will, so **he, in his architecture, sought to make the images of flow a fact, to celebrate continuous space, and to bring all together into shapes which were unified by his will**. . . . This image of "continuous becoming," as of the river, the sea, or the prairie, was a constant in Wright's work.

—Vincent Scully, Jr., architecture historian

**[To] get the essential character of an organic building . . . is wholly a matter of experience. One must be *in* the building before he can understand what makes it what it is.** . . . [This] building living before us now as an organism (twentieth century) may only be seen *by experience within* the actual structure. . . . Profoundly natural, these buildings are never dull or monotonous because this subtle quality of integrity due to "the each in each and the each in all" is continually there although not tangible to any superficial view. The essence of organic building is space, space flowing outward, space flowing inward (not necessarily by the use of the picture-window). Both plan and construction are seen to be inspired from within. . . . Only when the buildings are comprehended from within and each in its place a feature of its own special environment— serving its own appropriate purpose with integrity—are they really seen.

—Frank Lloyd Wright, 1957

What is extraordinary about this building is that it does two things at the same time. You know, architects always talk about defining spaces. So they define space with walls, they define space with glass, with a lot of things. In other words, they make boxes or containers or cylinders or whatever. And then they talk about activating the space—in other words, moving through that space via stairs, walkways, bridges, etc. They rarely succeed in doing what this building does: it simultaneously defines and activates the same space at the same time. Because **at the Guggenheim, it's the movement of bodies in space that defines that space**.

—Bernard Tschumi, architect, New York City

**Beyond all else it is truly an exceptional venue for an opening, wherein the art aficionados may represent themselves to themselves.** I know of no better public room where aside from the festive presence of art, the space becomes, however momentarily, a narcissistic whirlpool, where the main aim, in the seemingly endless promenade, is to see and be seen.

—Kenneth Frampton, architecture historian

**I love this building** *empty.* The emptiness and the light, the shadows, create a mysterious feeling. I would love to walk through this empty museum, hear the steps reverberate in the hollowness of the space. **I love this building** *occupied*, creating always a celebratory feeling. A celebration of Art and Architecture.

—Diana Agrest, architect, New York City

The building as a whole offers many strange and significant effects. Upon entrance, . . . the building seems small. It does not exalt man standing fixed and upright within it. **The meaning is in the journey, since from above, upon leaving the elevator, the visitor finds the space dizzying and vast, while the great downward coil of the ramp insistently invites him to movement.** Upon arriving at the ground floor once more, he will find that the building seems much larger than before because the long journey through it is remembered. But as that memory fades, the heavy vertical piers . . . , the dome struts, and the bright side-lights catch his eye and reduce the space in size once more, so that he must move again soon if the sensation of freedom and vastness is to be regained. Thus he is kept, in all truth, "on the road."

—Vincent Scully, Jr., architecture historian

I'm not a Frank Lloyd Wright fan. That having been said, I think the Guggenheim Museum in New York is one of the great buildings in our time. . . . What I find so interesting about the Guggenheim is how it displaces the relationship between the viewer, the person looking at paintings, and the paintings—how paintings now have to be seen as objects with people. In other words, you look across the views, and you see not just paintings, but you see people and paintings. **Wherever you look, you're always looking at people, architecture, space, and painting; and it's an amazing juxtaposition as opposed to the traditional museum.** You're also seeing them standing on one foot or another foot but never level, which displaces the normal relationship between the body and the vertical plane of hanging pictures. The space vibrates in the sense that it goes from narrow to wide. I think it is an extraordinary achievement.

—Peter Eisenman, architect, New York City

If the open spaces of MoMA and of museums by Mies represent Modernism's paradigm, Wright's spiral is its antithesis. . . . At the Guggenheim, Wright respected the classical museum typology of a central dome and grand stair (transformed by him into a ramp) and at the same time revolutionized the relationship between art, architecture and the viewer. . . . Wright emphasized movement as opposed to geometry. The Guggenheim's curvature freed paintings of rectilinear framing architecture; **the ramps and rotunda allowed viewers to observe each other as well as the exhibits from an unprecedented number of perspectives**. Long before the [Centre] Pompidou, it gave people an importance equal to that of the art for which it established a whole new environment.

—Victoria Newhouse, architecture historian

I know of no greater pleasure than to look at art in this space; this constant play between the close focus and the middle-distant view, this pleasant tension between the piece one is currently looking at, the piece one has just left behind and the piece that one will shortly see. What other modern museum has so succinctly captured the essence of "musing," for here surely one has it, the world of art and its public caught for an instant in a space-time vortex where past, present, and future find themselves suspended together for an illusory moment, in a single, spiraling continuum.

—Kenneth Frampton, architecture historian

It may not be the ideal model for the contemporary art museum, but the building has an autonomy that is equal to the great works of art—a building that is great art and great architecture in itself and thus challenges any content to be equally superior and forces a dialogue between container and content; it provokes a dialectic between art and architecture, between object and space.

—Hans Hollein, architect, Frankfurt

Repeated exposure to the Museum reveals the unimportance of the element of novelty in the experience. Once the shock of our own unusual situation passes, we begin to sense the challenge of the building as a momentous architectural event, in which movement takes possession of a big, unified, molded space, not simply by occurring within it, but literally by making it. . . . The space does not merely ask for the "make do" of compromise between museum practices and the exceptional character of the building; it forces a reconsideration of old ways of doing things in the necessity of coming to terms with what is. . . . Certainly architectural space will become more extravagantly sculptural. Surely, then, painting and sculpture will change with it, as contrariwise, modern painting and sculpture have already transformed architecture.

—William H. Jordy, architecture historian

Since its inception, Wright's spatial accomplishment at the Guggenheim has not been rivaled. Perhaps for this reason it seems, for me, **further ahead of its time today than it did when it was first built**.

—William Pederson, architect, New York City

I have always felt, despite criticism to the contrary, that the rotunda, instead of being antithetical to art, invites creative installation intervention that reinforces the imposed counterpoint: that is, the dynamics of art and architecture out of context and norm.

—Charles Gwathmey, architect, New York City

After the middle of the twentieth century, artists tried some different, more dynamic directions, such as large-scale paintings or installation art—not just showing the object on its own, but in a specific environment or a particular space. And then video artists and other artists who used new technologies and products needed a new type of space to show their new kinds of art. These artists created art that Frank Lloyd Wright could never have imagined but that later would make this museum so interesting, because new types of art exhibitions could be shown here. . . . I think the Guggenheim has become a new model for the third-generation museum. This space provokes the artist, the living artist, when they try to do some activity inside it.

—Arata Isozaki, architect, Tokyo

The Guggenheim Museum and the Art of this Century

With regard to the Guggenheim Museum as a key work of Wright, I must say it is not one of my favorites. . . . Notwithstanding, [it] is one of the world's extraordinary buildings in terms of its spatial inventions, its formal wizardry, unforgettable image, and, more recently, for its **prophetic concept of a museum interior**.

—James Wines, architect, New York City

Frank Lloyd Wright, the great American anarchist, once wrote: "Palladio? Bramante? Sansovino? Sculptors . . . them all! Here is now, instead, Frank Lloyd Wright, the Weaver." Weaver of utopian, never-ending spirals; from the very core of the earth up to the azimuth. The Guggenheim Museum is just a bit of it. A museum where the work of art is not contemplated; curved walls, sloping walls, but then, **just because of the opposition, inexorable and continuous, between architecture and work of art, it can make their relation break out in a powerful and perfect way**

—Gae Aulenti, architect, Milan

Is the Guggenheim not, after all, the eternal revolutionary call of Architecture for a vortex that would gather into its empty center the dispersed energies of art and money in order to transmute them—through the signature of one—into a tomb of the Void? **After F. L. Wright's Guggenheim, all voids resonate in a counterpoint to texts, rituals, and to now indecipherable names.**

—Daniel Libeskind, architect, Berlin

**Begun as a building exclusively to show painting of a very specialized type, it ultimately came to exhibit forms of art that were neither painting nor sculpture of the traditional sort.** Sometimes it has been difficult to say whether it has simply adapted well to these new forms of expression or whether it has actually played some role in their creation. One of Donald Judd's first "contextual" works, for instance, was a site-specific piece for a Guggenheim International exhibition (1971). . . . Artists as diverse as Mario Merz, Robert Morris, Carl Andre, Dan Flavin, and Jenny Holzer have all been challenged by the building to produce new work. If the move to the shaped canvas by so many artists in the 1960s seemed in some sense justified by the space of the recently opened Guggenheim, certain large-scale Earthworks like Smithson's *Spiral Jetty* (1969–70) are difficult to imagine without taking Wright's structure into account.

—Neil Levine, architecture historian

The Guggenheim Museum belongs to those select few buildings whose importance grow as they age. **By defying the conventional, Frank Lloyd Wright has created a great building, not least a museum that requires the same invention in using it.**

—Helmut Jahn, architect, Chicago

# PHOTO CAPTIONS AND CREDITS

**cover** Façade of the great rotunda (detail), 1992. Photo by David Heald.

**endpapers** The "Night Rendering," ca. 1950–51 (detail), Wright's tempera-and-ink perspective of the Guggenheim Museum bathed in light and color, an intermediate version between his first sketches in 1943 and the groundbreaking on Fifth Avenue in 1956. Collection Peter Lawson-Johnston, New York.

**frontispiece** Wright sitting next to a model of the Guggenheim Museum in 1953 in the temporary pavilion he designed for a touring exhibition of his work, *Sixty Years of Living Architecture*, built on the future site of the museum. Photo by Pedro Guerrero.

**pages 4–5** Aerial view of Manhattan's Upper East Side, showing the Guggenheim Museum in its urban context, with the Central Park reservoir in the foreground, 1993. Photo by David Heald.

**page 7** View of the Guggenheim Museum from Central Park, ca. 1960. Photo by Robert E. Mates.

**page 8** View of the Guggenheim Museum and adjacent buildings, looking south on Fifth Avenue, ca. 1959. Photo by William Short.

**page 11** View of the great rotunda and the "bridge" to the small rotunda (now the Thannhauser Building, which Wright had called the "Monitor") during the *Dan Flavin* exhibition, 1992. Photo by David Heald.

**page 12** Façade of the great rotunda (detail), 1992. Photo by David Heald.

**page 17** Interior of the great rotunda, looking up toward the skylight, 1992. Photo by David Heald.

**page 18** Stairwell, 1992. Photo by David Heald.

**page 20** Interior of the small rotunda, looking up toward its skylight, 1992. Photo by David Heald.

**page 21** Interior of the small rotunda at its highest level, showing its skylight and its windows onto the terrace overlooking Central Park, 1992. Photo by David Heald.

**page 22** Ramp of the great rotunda (detail), 1992. Photo by David Heald.

**page 25** Interior of the great rotunda during the exhibition *China: 5,000 Years*, 1998, with installation design by Arata Isozaki. Photo by Ellen Labenski.

**page 26** *Midsummer Circles*, 1993, a sculpture by Richard Long at the top of the rotunda ramp during the *Nasher Collection* exhibition, 1997. Photo by Ellen Labenski.

**page 27** Interior of the small rotunda with sculptures by Louise Bourgeois, *Femme Volage*, 1951 (left) and *Dagger Child*, 1947–49, during *The Global Guggenheim* exhibition, 2001. Photo by Ellen Labenski.

**page 29** View of the rotunda ramp during the exhibition *Forty Modern Masters*, 1977. Photo by Robert E. Mates.

**page 30** Ramp of the great rotunda (detail), 1992. Photo by David Heald.

**page 33** Interior of the great rotunda during the inaugural exhibition, October 1959, with sculptures by Constantin Brancusi in the foreground and on a pedestal in the middle of the floor. Photo by Ezra Stoller © Esto.

**page 34** People strolling down the rotunda ramp during the *Picasso and the Age of Iron* opening, March 1993. Photo by Lee Ewing.

**page 37** People mingling on the ground floor during the inaugural exhibition, October 1959. Photo by Robert E. Mates.

**pages 38–39** Architects and other guests attending an evening in tribute to Frank Lloyd Wright on the occasion of the 125th anniversary of his birth and the reopening of the museum after renovation, June 24, 1992, featuring a site-specific work by Dan Flavin. Photo by David Heald.

**page 41** Interior of the great rotunda before the museum's opening in October 1959. Photo by Ezra Stoller © Esto.

**page 42** Interior of the great rotunda, with a sculpture by Auguste Rodin, *Walking Man*, 1900, on top of a marble column in the exhibition *1900: Art at the Crossroads*, 2000. Photo by Ellen Labenski.

**page 45** People looking at paintings by Pierre Bonnard, Joan Miró, and Vasily Kandinsky, among others, in the bays of the rotunda ramp during the inaugural exhibition, October 1959. Photo by Ezra Stoller © Esto.

**page 46** Interior of the great rotunda looking up toward the skylight, with a sculpture by Claes Oldenburg and Coosje van Bruggen (hanging over ramp railing) and a mobile by Alexander Calder (suspended below skylight) in *The Global Guggenheim* exhibition, 2001. Photo by Ellen Labenski.

**page 48** The High Gallery transformed by Lothar Baumgarten's installation *AMERICA Invention*, 1993. Photo by David Heald.

**page 49** Interior of the great rotunda looking down at the ground floor during *The Global Guggenheim* exhibition, 2001, featuring a sculpture by Richard Long on the ground floor and a mobile by Alexander Calder hanging from the skylight. Photo by Ellen Labenski.

**page 50** Paintings by Ellsworth Kelly viewed from the opposite side of the great rotunda during his retrospective, 1994. Photo by Sally Ritts.

**pages 52–53** A sculpture by Alberto Giacometti on the rotunda ramp during *The Global Guggenheim* exhibition, 2001. Photo by Ellen Labenski.

**page 55** The great rotunda during the *Alexander Calder* retrospective, 1964, featuring two stabiles on the ground floor and mobiles suspended above them, and another stabile in the High Gallery. Photo by Robert E. Mates.

**page 58** View of the great rotunda transformed by architect Frank Gehry's installation of *The Art of the Motorcycle* exhibition, looking up toward the skylight, 1998. Photo by David Heald.

page 61  Interior of the great rotunda during the *Dan Flavin* exhibition, 1992. Photo by David Heald.

page 62  Installation by Nam June Paik (in collaboration with Norman Ballard) in the middle of the great rotunda during *The Worlds of Nam June Paik* exhibition, 2000. Photo by Ellen Labenski.

page 64  The top of the rotunda ramp with an installation of metal-mesh sculpture designed by Frank Gehry & Associates suspended from the skylight during the exhibition *Frank Gehry, Architect*, 2001. Photo by Ellen Labenski.

page 67  The great rotunda during Lothar Baumgarten's installation *AMERICA Invention*, 1993. Photo by David Heald.

page 68  Jenny Holzer's L.E.D. signs along the insides of the great rotunda's parapet walls and seventeen of her marble benches arranged in a circle on the ground floor during her 1989 exhibition, viewed from the top of the rotunda ramp. Photo by David Heald.

page 71  Exterior of the great rotunda during the *Dan Flavin* exhibition, 1992. Photo by David Heald.

Many thanks go to Kimberly Bush, Manager of Photography and Permissions, for her assistance in researching photographs for this book.

## TEXT CITATIONS

foreword  The quotes are from Mies van der Rohe, "A Tribute to Frank Lloyd Wright (1910/1946)," *College Art Journal* 6 (autumn 1946), p. 42; and "Philip Johnson on Frank Lloyd Wright, an Interview," in *An American Genius: Frank Lloyd Wright* (New York: Philosophical Library, 1986), p. 47.

page 1  Calatrava, quoted in "The Architecture World Pays Tribute to Frank Lloyd Wright's Guggenheim," *Guggenheim Magazine* 5 (spring/summer 1994), p. 5.

page 2  Venturi, ibid., p. 7.

page 3  Scott Brown, ibid., p. 6.

page 6  Portzamparc, ibid., p. 4.

page 9  Eisenman, from an interview conducted by Paula Rackow in a symposium on the architecture of the Guggenheim Museum building, June 1–3, 2000, and subsequently edited for this publication.

page 10  Holl, quoted in "The Architecture World Pays Tribute" (see note to page 1, above), p. 5.

page 13  Neil Levine, *The Architecture of Frank Lloyd Wright* (Princeton, N.J.: Princeton University Press, 1996), p. 362, quoting Wright, *The Living City*, pp. 122, 240.

page 14  Anthony Alofsin, "Frank Lloyd Wright and Modernism," in *Frank Lloyd Wright: Architect*, exh. cat., ed. Terence Riley (New York: Museum of Modern Art, 1994), p. 51, summarizing and quoting Wright, "The Language of an Organic Architecture," in Wright's *The Future of Architecture* (New York: Horizon Press, 1953), pp. 320–24.

**page 15** Meier, quoted in "The Architecture World Pays Tribute" (see note to page 1, above), p. 5.

**page 16** John Coolidge, *Patrons and Architects: Designing Art Museums in the Twentieth Century* (Fort Worth: University of Texas Press, 1989), p. 43, quoting from "Frank Lloyd Wright's Sole Legacy to New York," *Interiors* 119, no. 5 (December 1959), p. 174.

**page 19** Wright, *The Japanese Print: An Interpretation* (Chicago: Ralph Fletcher Seymour, 1912), reprinted in Bruce Brooks Pfeiffer, *Frank Lloyd Wright: Collected Writings* (New York: Rizzoli, 1992), vol. 1, p. 117.

**page 23** William H. Jordy, *American Buildings and Their Architects*, vol. 5: *The Impact of European Modernism in the Mid-Twentieth Century* (New York and Oxford: Oxford University Press, 1972), p. 359.

**page 24** Isozaki, from an interview conducted by Paula Rackow (see note to page 9, above), and subsequently edited for this publication.

**page 28** Herbert Muschamp, *Man About Town: Frank Lloyd Wright in New York City* (Cambridge: MIT Press, 1983), pp. 116–17.

**page 31** Vincent Scully, Jr., *Frank Lloyd Wright* (New York: George Braziller, 1960, rpt. 1977), p. 11.

**page 32** Wright, *A Testament* (New York: Horizon Press: 1957), p. 232.

**page 35** Tschumi, from an interview conducted by Paula Rackow (see note to page 9, above), and subsequently edited for this publication.

**page 36** Frampton, quoted in "The Architecture World Pays Tribute" (see note to page 1, above), p. 6.

**page 40** Agrest, ibid., p. 4.

**page 43** Scully, *Frank Lloyd Wright*, p. 31.

**page 44** Eisenman, from an interview conducted by Paula Rackow (see note to page 9, above), and subsequently edited for this publication.

**page 47** Victoria Newhouse, *Towards a New Museum* (New York: Monacelli Press, 1998), pp. 220–21.

**page 51** Frampton, quoted in "The Architecture World Pays Tribute" (see note to page 1, above), p. 6.

**page 54** Hollein, ibid., p. 4.

**page 56** Jordy, *The Impact of European Modernism*, p. 352.

**page 57** Pederson, quoted in "The Architecture World Pays Tribute" (see note to page 1, above), p. 7.

**page 59** Gwathmey, ibid., p. 5.

**page 60** Isozaki, from an interview conducted by Paula Rackow (see note to page 9, above), and subsequently edited for this publication.

**page 63** Wines, "The Architecture World Pays Tribute" (see note to page 1, above), p. 7.

**page 65** Aulenti, ibid., pp. 3–4.

**page 66** Libeskind, ibid., p. 6.

**page 69** Levine, *The Architecture of Frank Lloyd Wright*, p. 361.

**page 70** Jahn, quoted in "The Architecture World Pays Tribute" (see note to page 1, above), p. 7.

**back cover** Paul Goldberger, "The Guggenheim Effect," *Guggenheim Magazine* 13 (fall 1999), p. 47.

*Frank Lloyd Wright's Guggenheim Museum:*
*An Architectural Appreciation*
© 2002 The Solomon R. Guggenheim Foundation,
New York. All rights reserved

Designed by Amy Henderson

Guggenheim Museum Publications
1071 Fifth Avenue
New York, New York 10128

Printed in Barcelona, Spain, by SYL

ISBN: 0-89207-260-1

Cover photo by David Heald